SAFE MONEY™

Taking Risk Out Of Your Retirement

Anthony R. Trupiano

Safe Money™

Published by:
90-Minute Books
Newinformation Inc
302 Martinique Drive
Winter Haven, FL 33884
www.90minutebooks.com

Published in the United States of America

ISBN-13: 978-0692429587
ISBN-10: 0692429581

For more information on 90-Minute Books including finding out how you can publish your own lead generating book, visit www.90minutebook.com or call (863) 318-0464

Here's What's Inside...

Dedicated to my beautiful wife Sally and daughters, Jessica and Brianna who support me no matter what I do. They make my life the masterpiece it is by just being a part of it and loving me unconditionally.

Also to my twin brother John, we survived the loss of our father at a young age by always having each other's backs. He also helped me through college and will always be an important part of my life.

Lastly, this book would not be possible without the unwavering support of our clients. They believe in our Safe Money™ philosophy without question and have continued to support our efforts by continued referrals, speaking highly of us and placing their money in our care. We take our job very seriously when it comes to managing our client's money; they count on us to do the right thing and we promise to always put their interests first.

WHAT IS SAFE MONEY™?

Safe – Protected from or not exposed to danger or risk; not likely to be harmed or lost.

Money – The assets, property and resources owned by someone or something; wealth.

Above are the definitions of **SAFE MONEY™**, however it goes beyond definitions, it is our planning philosophy and our well designed proprietary planning process. It addresses all 5 major risks we believe exist for every individual and/or family in America.

1. **Global Risk**
2. **Market Risk**
3. **Longevity Risk**
4. **Healthcare Risk**
5. **Family Continuation Risk**

Released May 2015
Sanford, FL

My father passed away of heart failure at age 45 without life insurance or a retirement plan, which left our family broke and destitute without warning. I was only 16 years old at the time, but it affected the way I live my life to this day, empowering me to learn how to protect my family and my wealth and to ensure every family I touch avoids the pitfalls our family experienced. I feel I have an ethical obligation to help others understand how to retire safely and not be one of the 9 out of 10 retirees who are dependent upon the government, their families, or working for the rest of their lives.

My goal is to help people avoid being the thermometer that changes every time the market moves up and down. I want them to become a thermostat and learn how to control their own destinies. The financial world has changed so much in the past two decades with the introduction of derivatives (I explain what this means in the book!) and increased use of mutual-fund-based products that could completely destroy a person's retirement plan. I share how using Safe Money Solutions™ can give you and your family a **PREDICTABLE and SAFE** retirement solution.

The wealthiest 1% will still be wealthy when the market collapses next.

The poorest 15% living in poverty will still be poor when the market collapses next.

The 84% of Americans in the middle are the audience for this book, as they will be in trouble when the market collapses next.

Things are always good until they are not good anymore, and that is when you wish you had SAFE MONEY™!

Enjoy the book!

I hope this book both educates and empowers you to take control of your own destiny, changing the way you think about retirement planning and keeping your money safe.

To Your Success!

Anthony R. Trupiano

TRUPIANO & ASSOCIATES

SAFE MONEY SOLUTIONS
PROTECTION & GROWTH

Why More Retirees Don't Enjoy Risk-Free Retirements

We insure our houses, our cars, our health and even some insure their jewelry, but why not insure your retirement accounts, are they not as important to you?

Most people are unaware of how risky their investments are and how much of their hard-earned money is lost in fees. They lack the knowledge of how to protect their downside without the fees and set up guaranteed income for life.

People never think to protect their downside when it comes to their retirement. Why isn't retirees' money being kept safe? One main reason is that much of the fees embedded in the products on the market are hidden or not fully disclosed. As a result, there's a lot of confusion on how to protect your assets.

I also see people being lied to when told what is a reasonable rate of return. You hear a lot of financial services agents saying, "You have to beat out inflation, increase your risk." I don't think a retiree or someone leading up to retirement understands that by doing so they are increasing their risk exponentially, not linearly, and this increases the risk of failure. The greater risk, therefore, doesn't translate into higher return. It actually equals more failure for them.

The risk most people are undertaking is unnecessary. That's a main reason I wanted to write this book. I want to get people to see, first of all, how much risk they are really taking and, second of all, to show them there is a better way to ensure they get the retirement they want but without the downside – without the risk.

Most people have very little knowledge about the strength of a company or where to invest, and they are probably embarrassed to admit that they have no knowledge of how to properly review an investment or the company behind the investment.

An issue that gets in the way of a successful retirement is withdrawing too much money during the retirement years. Most people, when they finally get to retirement, view every day as Saturday. They have a lump sum of money, and they don't know how to manage it throughout their retirement years so that it lasts during this period of time.

Another reason people encounter problems in retirement is because, and I know it's going to sound funny, but they don't know how to fire their current broker or agent.

Often, when we do research on someone's current financial situation, we see that their investments are underperforming, their fees are too high, or they are involved with the wrong investments. But even in the face of all the evidence, they don't want to get rid of their current advisor because they think their advisor is a nice person. As silly as that is, they are worried about firing their nice agent even though they're not doing their job and putting their client's future at risk.

Most people are just taking on entirely too much risk, and they don't understand how the Standard Deviation affects their investment. Standard deviation means that in any given year an investment could go up or down by a certain percentage. They could experience a gain, or they could experience a loss. A bank CD or a money market account really has no standard deviation; they're guaranteed accounts, but when you start looking at stocks, bonds, mutual funds, and ETF's, they have a standard deviation or a risk rating. As an example the Standard deviation on the popular S&P 500 index is 17, meaning it could go up or down 17% in any given year historically.

Honestly, most advisors don't even know what the standard deviation is on an investment, and they don't know how to explain it to their clients. The more they are risking, the higher their chance of failure, and the years 2008 and 2009 are a great example of this. There was a $14 trillion loss when the stock market crashed. The market went down by 55%. A lot of people haven't recovered from it to this day. Even though the market is back up, they lost all their purchasing power. In order for the market to return to break even it took an increase in the market of 122.2% due to loss of purchasing power, see chart on next page.

Breakeven Chart	
Gain Required to Breakeven	
If You Lose:	To Breakeven:
5%	5%
[redacted]	[redacted]
15%	18%
20%	25%
25%	33%
30%	43%
35%	54%
40%	67%
45%	82%
50%	100%
75%	300%
90%	900%

An interesting survey was conducted on the top 12 billionaire investors, and it uncovered that their number-one rule was to protect their downside and avoid losing money at any cost. They use a formula that we use with our clients. It sounds fancy, but it's really simple, we call it "Asymmetric Investment Planning." Asymmetric investing is when the gains and the losses are not even. Like most millionaires and billionaires, they figure out how important it is to protect their downside and capture all upside.

While Millionaires and Billionaires use this asymmetric model to capture all the upside and avoid having any downside. The average investor gambles with their retirement while having no downside protection and loss of purchasing power. Whether it is the market crashing or false rates of returns are reported by mutual fund companies, most investor's accounts continue losing money because of little or no downside protection. Remaining in a poorly performing investment for long periods of time with hidden fees and risk makes it impossible for the average investor to accumulate enough for their retirement.

Most people think that their advisor is equally allocating risk by dividing their investments between Stocks and Bonds, however they are not. If a person is 50% stocks and 50% bonds, which is the average portfolio model used by most advisors, they're really 90% stocks and 10% bonds since stocks are 3 times riskier than bonds. Take a look at the charts on the next page; they show you the risk parity between stocks and bonds.

The Reality for Most Retirees

Nine out of 10 retirees will have to rely on the government, their families, or continued work in their retirement years. Sixty-five percent will have to continue to work until they die. The number-one fear for over 85% of retirees is that they're going to outlive their money. It's a huge concern; it's on everybody's minds. Relying on government subsidies is probably not a solid retirement plan or good long-term solution. To try and offset this, a lot of people will continue to ride the emotional rollercoaster of investing in the stock market and being subject to its ups and downs. All the while, the fees will continue to erode their gains.

What does it look like at retirement? Most people get to retirement with a lump sum of money, but they don't know what to do with it. They were used to getting a paycheck, or they had cash flow from owning their own business. Now they're staring at this huge investment, and they aren't equipped with how to manage it correctly. Part of what we do is turn our clients' accounts into guaranteed streams of lifetime income. This prevents the problem of a lump sum of money, which is very easy to overspend or mismanage.

Safe Isn't Sexy or Is It?

One of the reasons people need a new model for their retirement is because the world has shifted and changed over the last few decades. The dollar has lost its value due to inflation. Of course, there's a loss of purchasing power that goes along with that. When Social Security began, there were 10 workers to every 1 retiree. Today there are 3 workers to every 1 retiree, which makes a big difference in supporting Social Security burden. The Tax Equity and Fiscal Responsibility Act of 1982; opened the door to employers setting up 401(k) plans for employees versus providing costly pensions. Since the '80s, many investors have relied on the funds they had to pick from their 401(k) plans, or they have relied on advisors choosing the funds they should be in. Things are a lot more complex than they were even a few years ago.

Mutual funds have been an absolute disaster. There have been over 6,500 mutual fund failures and/or mergers from 2000 to present, that equates to an attrition rate of 85%.

It's not a safe place to keep money, but those are the choices that most investors have for their retirements in 401(k) plans.

Most people believe that "Safe isn't sexy." To most people, safe investments aren't sexy. When everyone is talking by the water cooler at work, they don't want to hear about someone who has been consistently earning 3% to 7% a year every year. They want to hear about the guy who said, "Oh, I doubled my money on this stock" or, "I earned over 20% in XY&Z investment." I think people are realizing the older they get and the closer they get to retirement that safe is, in fact, a lot sexier than being risky.

The #1 Concern for Retirees

The number one concern for retirees and for anyone getting close to retirement is that they will outlive their money. If you get to retirement and you're like most people, you will have to rely on the government or family. When you don't have your retirement handled, there is a loss of freedom in retirement. You watch these TV commercials from investment companies and they show someone golfing, vacationing, or spending time with their grandchildren, but that's not the reality for most retirees. Most will work until they become angels.

The reality is that 9 out of 10 people will still be working in their retirement years. They're going to rely on Social Security, which hasn't kept up with the cost of living. They're going to rely on family, which comes with a major loss of freedom and a lot of insecurity. With the way purchasing power is going, a lot of people are going to be very near poverty level.

When you look closer, these are not people who have just lived beyond their means. These are people who put away for retirement but exposed themselves to too much risk, in my opinion, which means now they don't get to enjoy their retirements like the financial industry TV commercials promote.

Let's take a closer look at how this unfolds. If you think about a person graduating college, let's just say the average age would be 22 years old. Maybe they went for their Master's degree, so they're closer to 25. They're going to work approximately 40 + years until retirement. The average retirement account is less than $101,000, based on Fidelity and Vanguard 401k balances, which is not enough money to last someone through retirement, let alone allow them to vacation and play golf every day. Even if somebody saved up a million dollars, which may sound like a lot, they could possibly live for another 30 years in retirement. People are definitely living longer, so even with a million dollars to work with, it's a stretch. Most people are simply underestimating what their needs are going to be when they retire.

Estimated Existing Average 401k Balances As Of March 31, 2013

Age Group	Amount
Gen Y (22-34)	$16,500
Gen X (35-48)	$63,600
Overall Average (Jan, 2014)	$101,650
Baby Boomers (50-67)	$126,900
All 55 & Over	$150,300

Source: Fidelity and Vanguard

Fifteen years ago, before we had the major market crash of 2008-2009, record high Government debt and all the global issues, I used to have people tell me, "I'm going to retire at 55." I don't hear anyone advocating that today for obvious reasons. Someone who worked from 25 to 55 has worked for 30 years, but they could live to be 85. Most think by saving 5% to 10% of their working year's income that they can enjoy 80-90% of what they used to make during retirement. If they worked for 30 years only saving 5% of what they earned, how do they expect to retire for the next 30 years and survive? There is absolutely no room for mistakes.

The numbers don't add up, do they? There are millions of people who are thinking that this formula works when it doesn't. Imagine if you had to live on $101,650 during your retirement years, not possible for most. Truth is that the average for all 401(k) providers is more near $60,000 average balance, very scary indeed.

Now you may understand more clearly how 90% of retirees will depend on Social Security, family, other Government assistance or just plain work until they become angels.

How to Avoid the Biggest Mistakes People Make with Their Retirement

One of the biggest mistakes people make with regard to their retirement is gambling with their retirement. Interestingly enough, some of our wealthiest clients are a lot more concerned about their money than someone who doesn't have a lot of money. Not sure why that is exactly, but I see it all the time.

You often hear other advisors recommending a "safe bucket" and a "risk bucket." I don't think a risk bucket belongs in anyone's retirement plan or at least make it a very small bucket. The trick is to think like billionaires do. The number-one rule for billionaires is protect your downside; don't lose money. I don't see why everyone shouldn't think the same way.

Another common mistake I see is a lot of employees who have 401(k) plans simply picking the funds each year based on which ones gave the best return in the year that they're in or based on the previous year's return. That's gambling with your future, and I think that's a big problem.

A major mistake most investors make is not firing an underperforming advisor because they like them personally. Successful people base their advisors on results, not likability. I know it can be hard to do, but do you want to risk your future with someone who is not keeping your money safe? Also find out if your advisor is personally invested in what he or she is recommending you invest in, fair enough right?

All this is based on personal experience. I had an offshore account in Bermuda where I lost my money, a precious metals account at the Perth Mint in Australia and never felt safe keeping anything there; also the service was horrible. We bought a home in 2000, within weeks after the Dot Com market crash. It took a large portion of our Vanguard S&P 500 Index Fund with it. I've been in risky products. I've been through the process. I'm not someone who is giving advice and hasn't been there. I've learned to put my oxygen mask on first, and I'm ready to help others avoid the same mistakes I've made.

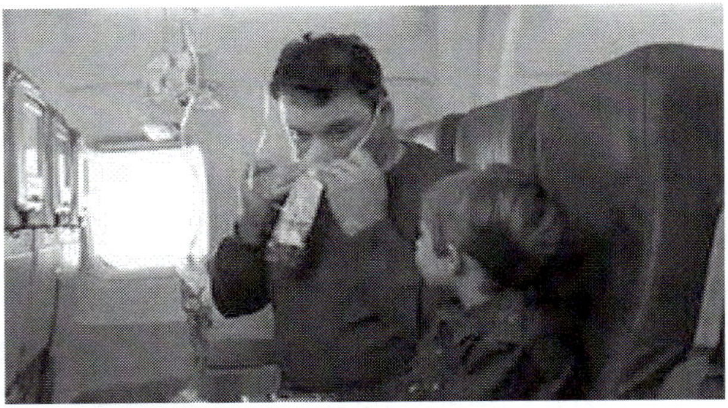

You go into any bank branch nowadays, and they have financial advisors practically harassing customers standing in line who just want to make a simple deposit or withdrawal. They want to sit down and talk to you about a new credit card offer or a new investment they just made available. The industry sells a lot of variable products that are mutual-fund-based, stock-based, or bond-based, and these are not safe investments. They tell you to keep your money with them over the long run while they keep charging fees on a monthly or annual basis.

Most advisors suggest allocating your risk. They will suggest putting some into a high-risk fund and keeping some in bonds. These mixtures simply do not work as I previously mentioned regarding risk parity.

Dalbar Study did a study over 30 years of equity funds, blended funds, and fixed-income funds. The return for equity funds over 30 years was 3.69%. The blended funds were 1.9%, and the fixed-income funds were less than 1% and more like 0.7%. There's a money illusion out there. Wall Street and most financial advisors that work for companies or brokerages tell everyone that they should be earning 8% to 12% consistently.

In fact, in our industry, you are allowed to illustrate an investment up to 12% legally, but it's not the reality. I could pull ratings for 750 very big, very smart insurance companies around the world and look at their industry average returns on assets; their average return on their assets is 5.05%. I don't know why anyone would expect returns near double that of the insurance industry with their certified financial planners, brokers or agents. The truth is, that kind of return just doesn't exist without a lot of risk and fees.

I want to open everyone's eyes to the truth about how much risk they are taking on and show them that there is a better way. There is a way to keep your money safe *and* have the retirement you dreamed of become a reality.

Exposing Common Financial Myths

Myth #1 – Banks are a safe place to keep your money, and the FDIC is able to insure your account.

The truth is that the FDIC is way over-leveraged and can only insure about $5 for every $10,000 in the bank. There have been 538 bank failures since 2000. People ask me when the FDIC is required to pay account holders their insured amounts, this is going to sound ridiculous, however the law states **"As soon as possible."** Yes, the FDIC's responsibility to pay you back: as soon as possible.

Now recently in December of 2014, our President signed a Cromnibus spending bill that allowed the Banking industry to repeal a section of the Dodd-Frank Act, whereby derivative trading from the top banks is going to be insured by the FDIC and will have superiority over all other claims. Here is a great example of Wall Street being protected and Main Street being left unprotected.

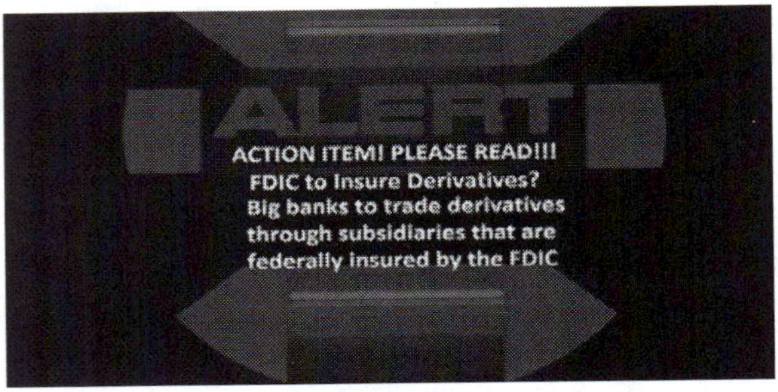

When someone deposits money in a bank, those funds become property of the bank, no longer yours. I get asked often what a derivative actually is; great question, however difficult to answer completely since very little is known about them and exactly how they work.

A derivative, put simply, is a contract between two parties whose value is determined by changes in the value of an underlying asset. Those assets could be bonds, equities, commodities or currencies. The majority of contracts are traded over the counter, where details about pricing, risk measurement and collateral, if any, are not available to the public.

In other words, a derivative does not have any intrinsic value. It is essentially a side bet. Most commonly, derivative contracts have to do with the movement of interest rates. But there are many, many other kinds of derivatives as well. People are betting on just about anything and everything that you can imagine, and Wall Street has been transformed into the largest casino in the history of the planet. After the last financial crisis, our politicians promised us that they would do something to get derivatives trading under control. But instead, the size of the derivatives bubble has reached a new record high, near 1.2 Quadrillion, nearly 20 times the GDP of all countries.

Companies in the financial and insurance industry are now using derivatives to leverage their required legal reserves or to back guarantees on products they are selling. This could cause a lot of problems when derivatives fail and most have zero knowledge of how this could wipe out their savings.

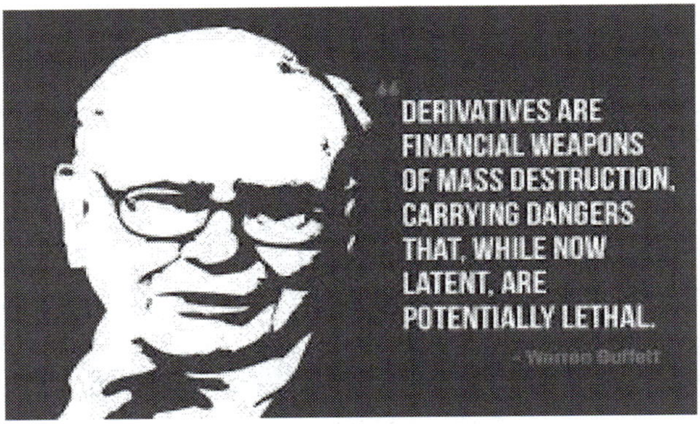

Credit unions seem to be safer than banks based on failure rates, however we believe Insurance contracts with a legal reserve company not using derivatives is the safest place to keep your money.

Myth #2 – Brokerage accounts are insured up to $500,000 by the Security Investor Protection Corp.

A lot of people make the mistake of thinking the SIPC will protect their brokerage account. The truth is, however, the SIPC is run by investment companies, and it does not insure one penny of market losses. It only insures against fraud. The fraud it covers is very limited; however, since it has a claw back provision that allows it to take back any of your distributions in the past six years if a Ponzi scheme was the cause of losses. The SIPC discovers about three to four Ponzi schemes a week, but we only hear of the large ones like Bernie Madoff or Allen Stanford.

To date Madoff investors have only recovered about 7 Billion of the over 65 Billion reported to be lost. They claim that it is closer to 10 Billion, however they include the increased IRS right offs for Madoff investors and the over 1 Billion in paid fees to the Wall Street law firms that represented the defrauded investors. So do not count on the $500,000 that the SIPC is supposedly telling you that you are insured for against fraud, because collecting the insurance is not easy or even a reality.

In a lesser know case involving a ponzi scheme about 9 months after Bernie Madoff was arrested. Allen Stanford, a Houston Texas based advisor, defrauded investors for approximately 7 billion dollars. The SIPC in this case went as far as hiring a team of high powered Wall Street attorneys and sued investors to not have to pay on their claims. The SIPC claimed it was not a security instrument Stanford was selling but rather a debt instrument and refused to insure the defrauded investors. By the way, over 200 of Stanford investors have passed away of old age and their families will never get a penny back.

Myth #3 – Mutual funds are safe and a great way to save for retirement.

This is a common myth as well. The truth is that 84.6% of mutual funds since 2000 have either been liquidated or merged, with over 2,000 failures since the 2008 market crash. In that same period they have increased their fees over 80%, and a lot of the fees are being hidden from investors.

A BREAKDOWN OF MUTUAL FUND FEES

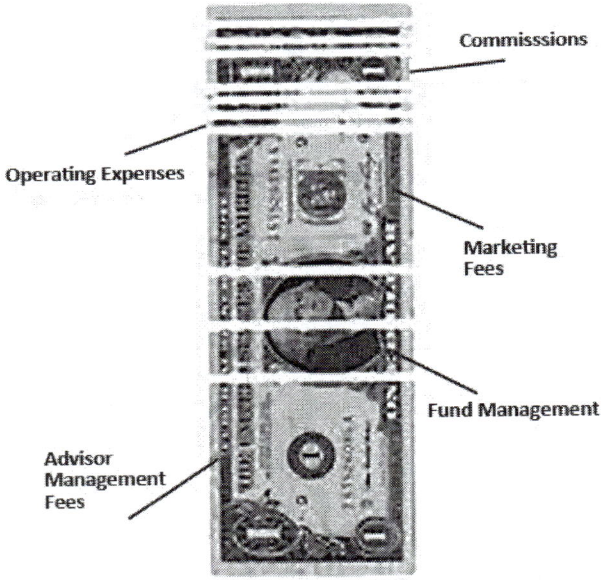

Myth #4 – Your pension plan is safe and secure.

The truth is that the Pension Benefit Guarantee Corporation has been in the red since 2002, they are broke, and unable to keep up with the increase in Baby Boomers requesting payouts. This is a disaster waiting to happen. Considering that over 25% of all mutual funds are held in pensions coupled with the PBGC in the red since 2002, it is a time bomb ready to explode.

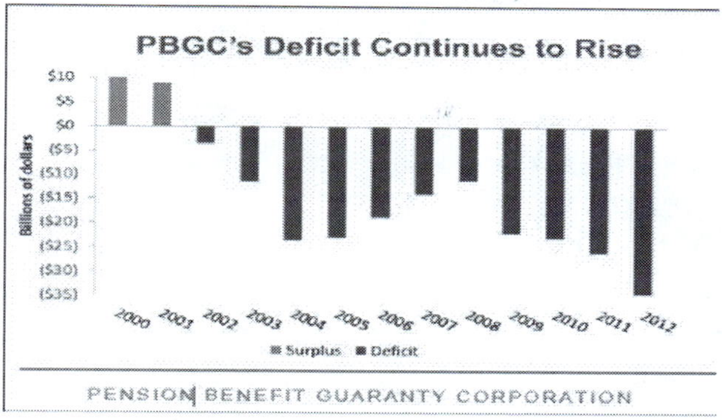

Myth #5 – Taxes will be lower during retirement.

Another big myth is thinking that taxes are going to be lower during retirement. They won't. Taxes keep increasing. People believe they'll use less money in retirement, but they're used to having a certain lifestyle while they're working and want to keep at least 80% to 90% of that lifestyle. They really need 80% to 90% of what they were making every year. So based on saving 5% of your income each year towards retirement, leaves no room for mistakes, risky investments, high fees and unnecessary taxes.

In some instances, retirees can have up to 85% of their Social Security payments taxed. Probably anyone reading this book that believes taxes are going lower are not currently paying any taxes.

Myth #6 – Invest for the long-run and use dollar cost averaging as a way to reduce risk and make money in the long run.

Brokerage accounts, 401(k) plans, and banks selling mutual fund products would love for investors to think long-term because they are like mosquitoes biting monthly at the account balance for collection of fees all while trying to keep the public worried about a bear market correction. Don't underestimate the damage that multiple mosquito bites can make, while knowing bear bites can be fatal.

The financial services industry makes billions of dollars in trail commissions and fees, so the longer you remain at a firm or bank, the longer they collect fees off of your account. They are still collecting their fees whether you make or lose money on your investments, certainly not a plan that I want to keep my money in.

Myth #7 – Unrealistic rates of return are attainable without risk.

This is completely untrue. The higher the return, the higher the risk. There is a money illusion that is being sold by the financial services industry of possible returns of 8% to 12% or higher; however, the reality is earning a predictable 3% to 7%. The average rate of return on assets for the entire insurance company industry is 5.05%, and these carriers on average hold less than 3% in stocks. However, the products they make most of their money on are the products with stocks or mutual funds, so they're not buying what they are selling. This is also true for the banking industry, which does not hold stocks or mutual funds as their tier-one capital because they are too risky. Just look at the Dalbar Study of Funds over 30 years.

Equity	Blended	Fixed Income	
10 Years	**5.88%**	**2.6%**	**0.6%**
20 Years	**5.02%**	**2.5%**	**0.7%**
30 Years	**3.69%**	**1.9%**	**0.7%**

***Study by Dalbar**

Quantitative Analysis Investor Behavior

Lastly, there is a reason why the insurance carrier and banks hold over 80% of their assets in highly rated or higher-rated bond portfolios. The best way for an individual investor to hold the same safe bond portfolio is via a fixed annuity contract with a carrier that is holding required legal reserves and not leveraged by risky derivatives.

Myth #8 – Retire with a lump sum of money that you can manage yourself through retirement years.

Instead, you must have guaranteed lifetime income balanced by taking 4% to 6% out annually, or your chances of running out of money exponentially increase. The 4% rule states that when taking over 4% of distributions from your retirement account annually it will increase the chances of running out of money exponentially. Reaching retirement and letting your lump sum sit in your account has become increasingly dangerous, as the most important aspect of retirement is guaranteed cash flow. Setting up your own guaranteed personal pension is what we strongly recommend our clients do, as every day is Saturday in retirement. Call it Murphy's Law, however it seems that your kids, grandchildren and every weird emergency you could think of, requires your savings once you retire. What you saved up during the years and worked so hard for should be protected and guaranteed to pay out for the rest of your life without worries of unexpected events wiping them out.

Myth #9 – Life insurance and long-term care are expensive and not affordable or necessary in retirement.

This is simply not true, since both forms of insurance are the best leveraged products to own in your Safe Money™ plan. Everybody thinks they're going to live forever or that they will never need long-term care, especially when family can take care of them. Life insurance really isn't that expensive, when using term insurance that can be converted into a permanent without repeating the medical approval process in most cases. Leaving your loved ones a tax free life insurance benefit can be life changing as to whether they maintain their current lifestyle or drastically change it.

Long-term care is used more often by women than men because women simply outlive men and underestimate what the cost of home care, let alone assisted living or facility care, will cost them. Long-term care in most cases involves a telephone interview and review of medical records; it doesn't involve having to go through the process of a full medical examination, like life insurance does. Some advisors will tell wealthy clients that they should self insure with their assets, but why when you can leverage your assets by using a quality long term care policy.

The Truth about 401(k) Plans

A lot of people put away in their 401(k) and IRA accounts to get the tax deduction. I tend to think of these plans as a tax deduction trap because it traps people into using only certain types of funds. An individual does have the power to choose what mutual funds they invest in, but the ultimate decision of what funds are even being offered to them is carried out by someone at their company who is probably not properly trained or someone at the 401(k) company who has a vested interest in picking the funds.

They are giving them a menu of funds, and most investors don't know to look at fees and they never list the standard deviation on each fund. They focus on the returns, what funds returned the most either last year or year to date, and those are the ones that they are choosing. They aren't thinking about what percentage is in stocks, bonds, or what's in the fixed account, and what the fees are. That's why I say they are gambling with their retirement. They might as well just close their eyes and pick funds randomly.

If people find themselves in this situation, we offer a complimentary service for clients and prospects: If they have a 401(k) at work and they still have time before retiring, we'll work with them on how to invest in that 401(k) based on the choices they're given in their employer sponsored 401(k) plan in order to keep it safe and grow based on their individual situation and or risk tolerance.

How to Keep Your Money Safe in Retirement

There is not one study that anyone can produce that proves taking on more risk is worth the investment. From 2000 to 2008, the stock market reached new heights, and then it crashed by 55%. Most had a decade of gains in the market completely erased in one swift market correction or at least pushed back to where they began.

Compare that to someone who earned 3% to 7% year in and year out, never had a loss, and just kept growing for that same decade. The investor that's going up and down in the market is never going to catch that person who has a safe-money bucket and keeps growing it. Below we have tracked our base of clients versus the S&P 500 index since we started our company in 2001. We needed to get a year of performance under our belts which is why the chart begins in 2002, however steady growth can clearly outperform unstable growth and just think about where the market stands now, a new high or next correction coming?

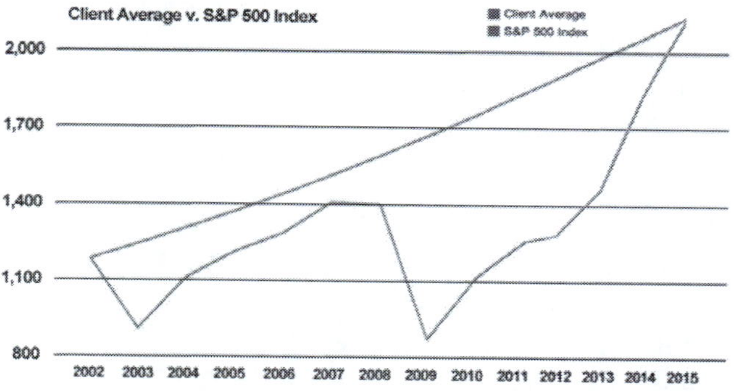

You need to make sure you are protecting your downside and you don't lose money. You need to be in an investment that has a reasonable rate of return. Now, when I say 'reasonable," I mean a bank will pay you less than 1% to keep your money there. In fact, it's almost like they are taxing you to store your money. They're going to start charging you fees to keep your money there. There are safe investments that will earn between 3% and 7%, a reasonable rate of return, with no fees.

PREDICTABILITY VS Possibility

We all like to gamble and win, but no one ever wants to talk about the losses and how devastating they can be. In Las Vegas, the house wins over 90% of the time, but 90% of your friends and family will tell you they won money. The same is true of Wall Street, the house makes money 90% of the time while most investors break even or lose money most of the time. Yes, investors do make money, however not what they really thought they would make and not without paying fees somewhere during the entire process.

The reason you don't see this information on the nightly news is because the media is controlled by the financial sector, the banks, and brokerage. As I mentioned before, there have been over 2,000 mutual fund failures since 2008 and 538 bank failures, but you've never heard about it on the news. No one talks about it because they control the media, and they do a really good job of controlling the information they want the general public to see and hear.

A great example of this is a mutual fund company and how they report their actual returns. If you had $100,000, and the mutual fund had a loss of -20%, the individual investor would be down to $80,000 in their account. But the next year, let's say it gains +20% for that same mutual fund. The mutual fund company is going to report that the two-year average on that fund is zero. It went down by -20% and then it went back up by +20%, so our 2-year average is 0, but the truth of the matter is that the individual investor went from $100,000 to $80,000, and then a gain of 20% on $80,000 only brought him up to $96,000; the investor actually suffered a loss of $4,000. If you analyze a mutual fund company reporting and twisting the truth like that for 20 or 30 years, their returns are going to look stellar compared to the truth of how they actually performed, don't you think you should know this?

How Billionaires Keep Their Money Safe

I like to use the billionaires Warren Buffett and Sir Richard Branson as examples because they are two totally different people. When you think of Warren Buffett, you think of a conservative Nebraskan guy. He buys into very safe investments; he owned insurance companies and railroads. He has his famous quotes like, "Rule number one: Don't lose money." Rule number two is, refer to rule number one. Warren Buffett has an image of being very conservative and safe.

On the flip side of that, Sir Richard Branson has the nickname "The Rebel Billionaire." He flies around in hot air balloons, drives fast speedboats, and opens up companies to go to outer space; in fact to the contrary, Sir Richard Branson's core business belief is: Protect the downside first. When he started his airline, Virgin Atlantic, he didn't even buy his planes; he leased them for one-year contracts, and he bought options on the fuel. He knew when he started his airline exactly what his costs were and what his downside was. He's anything but risky.

Sir Richard Branson looks risky on the outside, but his core belief is the same as Warren Buffett's and the same as the other 12 investor billionaires that I told you about. They all protect their downside first and foremost. They don't lose money. Individual investors don't engage in that same investing strategy, and it's not taught because big insurance companies, big brokerage companies, and Wall Street make money on investments that have a lot of risk and fees. That's what they sell but they don't own themselves. In fact, the average stock holdings in the Insurance Company industry is less than 3%, most of their holdings are invested in high quality bonds that you and I are not able to purchase. Think about a company as large as MetLife or MassMutual buying bonds in the millions, versus the average investor maybe buying a bond for a few thousand or even tens of thousands.

When I wrote my book "Insurance Lies," I did a study from 2002 to 2006 of mutual fund holders. It's amazing that 70% of mutual fund holders were the public. I believe about 25% were held in pension plans. And banks, credit unions, brokerage, insurance carriers and state/local government accounted for less than 5% in mutual funds. Meanwhile 80% to 90% of their products sold in the financial services industry use mutual funds as investments. The plain and simple truth is financial services industry is not buying what in fact they are selling or asking you to buy.

Keeping Your Money Safe Is Possible for Everyone in Any Market

I had a client in New Jersey whose mother and father-in-law lived next door. I believe he worked for the Sanitation Department in New York, and she was a teacher in New York. They had saved up a little over $3 million. In 2007 my client introduced me to them. I looked at their portfolio, keep in mind they were 80 years old and they had 87% of their portfolio invested in bank stocks. You can probably guess where this is going.

Now, the market was at 14,000 at this time, before the big crash in 2008. As a professional courtesy I contacted their advisor not wanting to take such a large account away from him and asked why at their age (80 years old) he had them invested so risky and would he consider moving them to more conservative investments. He actually told me I didn't know what I was talking about and that he truly believed the market would still continue higher, so they ended up moving their account to me. Had they left their account with that young man, they would have lost 55% of their wealth. That was about $1.7 million of their retirement. These stories exist a lot in our industry. This story had a happy ending, but they don't always end this way.

In September and October of 2008, the market crashed by close to 1,500 points, our phone wasn't ringing. I looked at my wife and said, "Wow, this is really strange. The market had the biggest correction since 2000, and no one is calling our office worried." I started picking up the phone and calling our oldest then largest clients, as I thought maybe they would be worried.

Every single client I called saying, "Hey, I just want to make sure you're not worried that the market is dropping" they all responded with, "No worries, we're not even concerned because we know you have our money protected. We know we are safe. In fact, we've been telling our friends that we didn't lose anything." What a great story to be able to share.

When Should You Begin Creating a Safe Money™ Retirement Plan?

People are living busier lives than ever before. We have a lot of demands on our time, and putting off planning for retirement is all too easy to do. I think people should really start to look at their retirement planning when they are around 35 years old.

Our industry tends to focus on retirees that are between 55 and 75. That's the demographic that seems to be the biggest target for advisors, but I think people by age 35 should start really seriously considering what they're going to do for retirement savings.

Understanding that most either entering the work force right out of high school or graduating college, they're just looking to make a living, get their career going, and then, of course, they're going to get married, buy a house, and have children. Retiring at 55 is not all that realistic for most people. Most people need to consider retiring at 65 or even 70. The average lifespan is now approaching 80 years old. As modern medicine continues to improve, we need to be prepared for an even longer retirement.

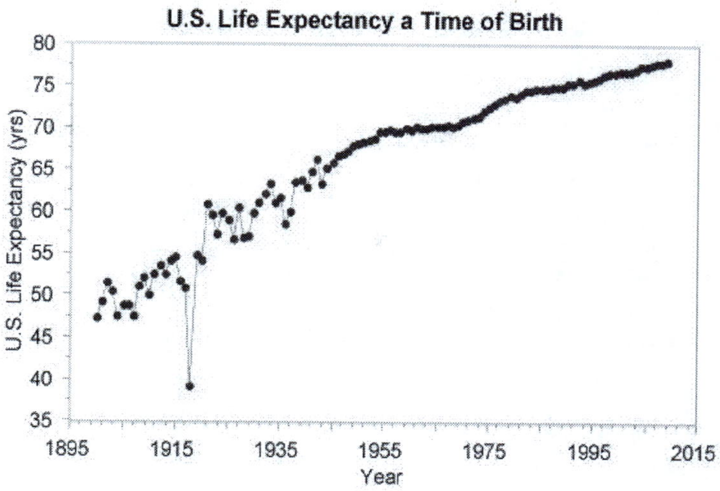
U.S. Life Expectancy a Time of Birth
U.S. Life Expectancy (yrs)
80
75
70
65
60
55
50
45
40
35
1895
1915
1935
1955
1975
1995
2015
Year

Find Out How At Risk Your Money Is

401(k) plans are infamous for being high in risk. When I look at most 401(k) plans for clients, I analyze all of the different mutual fund choices they are offered and consider fees and risk above performance. They don't realize that in most cases they are invested in 90% stocks, 10% bonds with nothing allocated to a fixed account. We do a complete risk assessment for our clients and then truly set up their 401(k) choices using a risk parity model.

We also obtain Bank ratings for our clients, showing them asset quality, liquidity and earnings for the banks they are currently using.

For insurance carrier ratings we use Vital Signs ratings and show them if the company they are currently with is safe or not. We can show carrier investment portfolios, average return on assets as well as their rating scores.

Comdex is a rating system that takes Moody's, Fitch, Am Best, Standard & Poor's and Weiss ratings, combines all the different agencies where these companies are rated, and gives them a total score. One hundred is the highest score a carrier can receive; obviously, below 70 is a poor score and below 50 is a concern. We won't go near a company unless they score 80 or higher on the Comdex ratings.

Here's a quick story to illustrate how important ratings are. It was between my company and a wealthy and prestigious broker up in the New York/New Jersey area for this particular client. I was recommending a Safe Money Solution™ to the client, and the other broker was recommending stocks. My client was leaning towards my solution and finally agreed to our recommendations. The other broker quickly turned around and said, "Well, I can do exactly what Anthony is doing." The return on the fixed product I was offering was 3%; the other broker claimed, "Well, I can get you 4% on the same type of product.

When I looked closer at his recommendation to my client, my company was ranked 92 out of 100 on a Comdex scale while his company was ranked 44 out of 100, not a company we would ever recommend to any of our clients and prospects.

The Dirty Little Secret the Financial World Doesn't Want You to Know

One of the dirty little secrets in the financial world is that there is no ethical obligation for Wall Street, banks, insurance companies or brokerage operations to make their clients money. In fact you will not find anything in writing that even obligates them to earn you money. They're paid from commissions and fees whether or not you earn a penny on your account.

When we look at companies, we're looking at their safety, whereas most agents are only looking at their commission. The solutions may be exactly the same, and yet you've got two different carriers. You have Carrier A and Carrier B. Carrier A is clearly the safer company, is better rated, has legal reserves, and is offering the same type of product, apples to apples, as Carrier B. Then you look at Carrier B, and their ratings are horrible. They are a very low-rated company selling the same product, but the agents are out there selling Carrier B's product to a client because they're getting another 1.5% to 2% commission. I wish it weren't true, but, unfortunately, this happens in our industry all the time.

That's part of what sets us apart. Other companies are just advocating entirely too much risk. They rave about the higher returns while failing to show the entire picture. Meanwhile it's not THEIR money at risk, it's the clients'.

Here's How to Take the Risk Out of Your Retirement

You already know that people are living longer than ever before. But how do you get the returns you need so you don't outlive your money…while avoiding all the risk?

That's where we come in. We help people just like you keep their money safe while providing the guaranteed lifetime income they need. We are in the business of **sharing predictability**, because your retirement is that important to us.

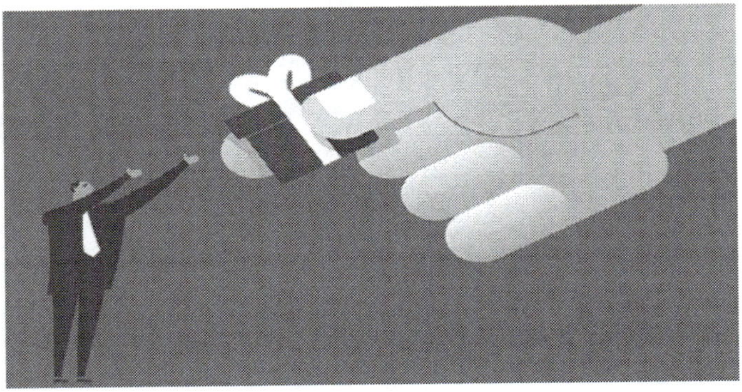

We work with clients from across the country. With today's technology, we communicate via phone, fax, text, email, scan, so we're able to work with anyone anywhere in the country.

Step 1: We meet with you for a one-on-one **Safe Money Consultation™** so we can see where you are right now and find out what you truly need to retire securely. Long-distance prospects can schedule **Safe Money™** conference calls with our office, as we are licensed to work nationwide.

Step 2: We then develop your **Safe Money Plan,** which will give you a road map to a safe retirement with guaranteed income strategies while protecting you and your family.

Step 3: We work with you on an ongoing basis, implementing each aspect of your **Safe Money Plan** one item at a time so the process is easy to understand and fits in your busy schedule.

Most people think it takes risking their hard-earned money in the stock market to get the returns they think they need to retire well; however, nothing could be further from the truth.

Now you can take the risk out of your retirement, and keep your money safe!

If you'd like us to help you, just send an email to **info@safe-money-solutions.com**, or please contact us at **1-866-640-7897**, and we invite you to join our **Safe Money™** family today!

Made in the USA
Monee, IL
04 November 2026

67386099R00026